HAWKER HURRICANE

Part Two: UK Based Fighters/Bombers Nov 1940 - Dec 1942

NEIL ROBINSON

Mk Is AFTER THE BATTLE

A symbolic photo of the standard Battle of Britain Hurricane Mk I being painted in post-Battle of Britain identification markings.

Introduced in late November 1940, these i/d markings included the propeller spinner and an 18 inch wide rear fuselage band being painted 'Sky' (or invariably a variation of Sky), and the under surface of the port wing being painted in Special Night (black) distemper with the roundel having an added outer yellow ring. V7048, has its earlier 'blunt' ES/6 Rotol propeller spinner painted in Sky and most of the port wing under surfaces (up to the main-wheel bay) in black. The rear fuselage band is still to be added. V7048 was delivered with an aerial wire running between the small mast on the rudder (A) and the main mast (B) which had a triangular attachment (C) to send the wire into the fuselage at (D). This was for the early TR9 radio, which was soon replaced by the much improved TR1133 VHF radio, that didn't need the aerial wire. Most aircraft in this book have the triangular attachment and rudder mast removed.

Right: Another big change at the end of the Battle was the introduction of a new and longer Rotol spinner, as seen on 615 Squadron Hurricane Mk I, V7017, KW•M in the background. These Hurricanes are still in the standard Battle of Britain markings of black spinner and Sky undersides.

Photographed here in late 1940, after the markings change, the veteran pilots of 249 Squadron pose grimly for the press. The mixture of old and new spinners can clearly be seen. The nearest Hurricane is a new Mk II, identified by the five equally spaced fasteners on the cowling panel (arrowed). The Mk I (opposite page) had only four fasteners, the first two of which were closer together. This was the result of the Mk II having a slightly longer nose to accommodate the more powerful engine.

Inset: There were two types of 'pointed' spinner introduced at this time, either the ES/9 or the slightly longer CM/1 – the difference in shape between the two is very subtle with the ES/9 having a constantly increasing curve from the back plate to the nose while the CM/1 has a flatter curve from backing plate to just in front of the blades and then a slightly steeper curve from that point.

Left: A 238 Squadron Mk I, fitted with a 'blunt' ES/6 Rotol propeller spinner, painted Sky or Sky Blue, with Jablo wooden propeller blades. In this instance, the Special Night (black) port wing under surfaces appear to have been correctly applied, extending to the aircraft's centreline. The uneven upper/under demarcation on the cowling is interesting.

Below: Flying Officer Whitney Straight, (a famous American pre-war civil aviator and racing car driver), and ground crew in front of his 601 Squadron Mk I at Northolt in February 1941. The 'pointed' Rotol propeller spinner and rear fuselage band have been painted in Sky. The port wing under surface is Special Night, but apparently only up to the main-wheel bay (arrowed).

Above: A very tatty V6727 of 238 Squadron still with 'Sky' under surfaces, before having the Special Night paint applied. Note the serial number V6727 chalked on the engine cowling panels. The pilot is Robert Kings.

Main image: 111 Squadron Hurricane Mk Is at RAF Dyce, Aberdeenshire, where the unit had been sent to rest and train-up replacement pilots following losses during the Battle of Britain. The aircraft are dispersed in the snow during the hard winter of late 1940/early 1941. Both Hurricanes are fitted with 'blunt' ES/6 Rotol propeller spinners and symmetrical tip propeller blades. The Special Night paint under the port wings only extends to the main-wheel bay. The ground crew appear to have taken the path of least resistance when it came to painting the under-wing port roundel. Instead of carefully painting a yellow ring around it, they just left a large expanse of the original Sky colour as a border!

Inset: This Cyprus based Hurricane shows how the application of the black paint on the port wing looked like when only taken up to the edge of the centre section/wheel-bay.

Main image and right: Two photos of Hurricane Mk I, V7607 DT•H of 257 Squadron in the late 1940/1941 winter snow at Coltishall. V7607, a Gloster-built machine, was fitted with a 'pointed' Rotol propeller spinner and Jablo wooden blades.

Below: When 257 Squadron was re-formed in May 1940, it was the first RAF unit to be named as a 'gift squadron' (in honour of British territories that had provided funding to support the war effort). It was 'allocated' Burma – a province of British India until 1937, when it was granted an element of independence within the British Empire. The squadron's aircraft carried the Burmese ensign (incorporating a chinthe - the Burmese word for lion) under the cockpit.

Left: The CO of 257 Squadron during this period was Roland Robert (Bob) Stanford Tuck. He was posted to command the unit as Acting Squadron Leader in September 1940, a post he held until July 1941 when he was promoted to Acting Wing Commander of the Duxford Wing. Here, he is (centre) putting his parachute on with two other squadron pilots in front of one of the aircraft he flew, V6864 DT•A.

Tuck also flew V6555 and V6962, during this period, all from the same production batch built by the Gloster Aircraft Company Ltd at Brockworth, Gloucestershire, and delivered between early July and late November 1940. The line of small white swastikas under the cockpit appears to show twenty-five 'kills'. This dates the photo to after 29th December when Tuck claimed a Dornier Do 17 shot down over south east of Lowestoft. After this, he was awarded the DSO.

Main image: Three 257 Squadron Hurricanes taking off from Coltishall in early January 1941. Squadron Leader Tuck in (what is thought to be) V6864 leading Sgt Barnes in V6873 DT•O and P/O Pniak in V7137 DT•G. Tuck's and Barnes' Hurricanes were fitted with the 'blunt' Rotol spinner while Pniak's was fitted with the later 'pointed' Rotol spinner. All three aircraft have the black-painted underside to the port wing (unusually glossy on these aircraft), and a yellow ring around the roundel.

Top left: Squadron Leader 'Bob' Stanford Tuck probably in V6864, showing the Burmese ensign under the starboard side cockpit sill to good effect.

Top right and main image: Two starboard side views of V6864, probably taken during the same photo shoot, revealing further details of this aircraft. By this time, nearly all front-line Hurricanes were using the much improved TR1133 VHF radio, which didn't need an aerial wire running from the mast to the fin, so the triangular attachment point and the rudder mast have been removed (arrowed).

(See Modeller's Notes opposite for further details)

HURRICANE Mk I V6864 DT•A, 257 SQUADRON, JANUARY 1941

Modeller's notes

- V6864 was a Gloster-built machine produced at a time when Glosters were finishing the under surfaces of their Hurricanes in BS381 No 1 Sky Blue, rather than 'proper' Sky.

- To add to the confusion, the spinner and rear 18 inch wide fuselage band were finished in another shade of pale blue called RAE Sky Blue. The spinner tip was Roundel Red.

- The underside of the port wing was overpainted in black and terminated along the aircraft's centreline and fore and aft along adjacent transverse panel lines.

- Standard 8 inch high Night (black) serial numbers on the rear fuselage sides partially obscured by the RAE Sky Blue band (and squadron code letters), but repeated in approximately 2 inch high stencil style under the tailplanes.

- Twenty-five white swastika 'kill' markings (Tuck's score by 29 Dec).

- Burmese flag and 'BURMA' in white stencil style under starboard cockpit sill.

Discussion points

- Note how far to the rear the RAE Sky Blue fuselage band is, and truncated along the upper/under demarcation line.

- The leading edge of the fin is offset to port by 2°

Howard 'Cowboy' Blatchford climbing out of his 247 Sqn Hurricane at Martlesham Heath in mid-November 1940, just before the Sky spinners were applied.

This detailed photo shows many common Mk I features. A) are the two closely spaced fasteners on the bottom panel only seen on the Mk I. B) is the kick-in foot step, C) is the cover for the hand-hold and D) are the mounting holes for the exhaust glare shield. E) Is the transparent cover for the formation-keeping lamp. This lamp shone onto the trailing edge of the wing on both sides to aid formation flying in low light conditions. It first appeared on early P Series aircraft and was discontinued officially with Mod. 273.

Main image: Three 303 (Kosciuszko) Squadron Mk Is taking off from Leconfield. 303 moved to Leconfield (12 Group) in the East Riding of Yorkshire in October 1940 for a rest. It was common practice for rotating squadrons to swap aircraft, so two of these Hurricanes are older N Series aircraft, left behind by the squadrons that headed south. The aircraft taking off include N2460 RF•D, N2661 RF•J and RF•C whose serial number is unreadable.

Inset: The same three aircraft being readied for another sortie. Both N2460 and N2661 are fitted with a de Havilland propeller unit, but RF•C has the 'pointed' Rotol propeller spinner and Jablo wooden propeller blades. All three aircraft feature 'Sky' spinners and rear fuselage bands. None appear to have a yellow outlined roundel under the Special Night port wing, which again only extends to the main-wheel bay.

Being away from the front-line, these Hurricanes retain the older TR9 radio sets.

Far left: Another 'foreign-manned' unit equipped with Hurricanes in late 1940/early 1941 was 316 (City of Warsaw) Squadron. This was formed at Pembrey, South Wales, from Polish personnel in February 1941. V6735 SZ•B, was a Mk I with the Polish red/white chequerboard under the exhausts, and the Warsaw (Flying Owl) squadron badge behind the cockpit.

Near left: Another Polish-manned Hurricane unit was 315 (Deblinski) Squadron, formed in January 1941. P2827 PK•K, had served with four other squadrons before joining 315 in February 1941. It was retro-fitted with a 'pointed' Rotol spinner. The fuselage roundel has been repainted, as it would have been originally delivered with a very large blue/white/red roundel, of the type seen early in the Battle of Britain.

Above: Escaped Czechoslovak Air Force pilots formed 310 (Czech) Squadron in July 1940. Hurricane Mk I, W9323 NN•D joined the squadron in March 1941 and was photographed in the spring sporting a Sky 'pointed' Rotol spinner and accurately placed rear fuselage band. The port undercarriage door would indicate a truncated Special Night port wing under surface again.

Main photo: this UZ coded Mk I of 306 (Torun) Squadron, shows the different textures of the fabric covered tailplane and elevator nicely. Only the elevators and rudder were rib stitched, the ailerons, fin and tailplane had thin strips of alloy riveted into the structure to hold the fabric in place.

Also visible is the attachment point for the IFF wire (arrowed) that ran from the tailplane to the fuselage on both sides. This was introduced in early October 1940 and was fitted to all front line fighters and bombers as quickly as possible.

Above: V7066 of 312 (Czech) Squadron had its IFF fitted on the squadron, evidenced by the doped patch around the attachment point (A).

thin alloy strips

rib stitching (for strength)

Main image: Hurricane Mk I, V7608, XR•J of 71 Squadron was photographed in the spring 1941 after the squadron became operational at Kirton-in-Lindsey that February. V7608 had previously served with 253 and 303 Squadrons. It has a Sky 'pointed' Rotol CM/1 spinner and the rear fuselage band has been painted over the serial number. The Special Night port under-wing (with yellow outlined roundel) ends part-way across the main undercarriage bay. Note that the Hurricane in the background has its demarcation line (arrowed) further up the door at an angle that probably doesn't match the rest of the wing! The 'dark' area on the lower part of the u/c door is an oil stain, a common feature on all Hurricanes.

Inset: V7183 XR•W had also served with 253 and 303 Squadrons before it was allocated to 71 Squadron in February 1941. The RF code letters of its previous operator (303 Squadron) have been painted out and overlaid with 71's XR codes.

71 Squadron was re-formed at Church Fenton, North Yorkshire in September 1940, initially with Brewster Buffaloes. It rapidly re-equipped with Hurricane Mk Is, and became the first of three 'Eagle' squadrons, manned by volunteer pilots from the United States.

Main image: A pair of anonymous 71 Squadron Hurricanes taxiing out for take-off. Their serial numbers have been obscured by the rear fuselage bands.

Right: Hurricane Mk I, XR•Z (possibly V7606), looking 'well used', which, if it was V7606, it would have been. It had served with 253, 87 and 303 Squadrons before joining 71 Squadron in February 1941. V7606 was lost in action off Flamborough Head, East Yorkshire with its pilot, P/O Keough, while on convoy protection patrol on 15th February. The aircraft has a very individual camouflage scheme, which would be a challenge for any modeller to interpret!

Vernon 'Shorty' Keough from, Brooklyn, was 29-years-old, and the shortest pilot in the RAF at 4' 10".

EARLY NIGHT FIGHTERS

With German bombers roaming unhindered over the British Isles in the winter 1940, several Hurricane squadrons were tasked with 'having a go' at night fighting.

Inset above left: 255 Squadron had its night fighting Defiants supplemented with Hurricane Mk Is, of which V6793 YD•Z is an example. Finished in overall Special Night (RDM2), the aircraft also featured a red serial number, Medium Sea Grey codes and six-stack exhaust manifolds.

Main image: 87 Squadron's new C/O Ian 'Widge' Gleed landing his trusty P2798 LK•A, which was over-painted in Special Night (RDM2). The Medium Sea Grey codes were retained, although the individual aircraft letter 'A' was partially worn away, and the serial number was over-painted. The two parallel lines on the rudder are thought to be red doped repairs. P2798 was also fitted with six-stack exhaust manifolds.

Inset above right: Gleed made some additions to his markings including painting the 'blunt' Rotol propeller spinner red, with a matching red 'flash' on the cowling sides, and a Squadron Leader's pennant under the windscreen. This angle also shows that the aircraft retained its under-wing roundels.

Right: 'Widge' Gleed and 'Roddy' Rayner in front of another black-painted 87 Squadron Hurricane LK-B.

Top right: An intriguing shot of a 242 Squadron Mk II coded LE•Z probably photographed at Martlesham around March 1941. At this time the squadron embarked upon a short, unsuccessful, period of night fighting. The 'Sky' spinner, rear fuselage band and yellow outer ring of the fuselage roundel have been over-painted in black. Anti-glare shields have been fitted.

Middle right: 151 Squadron also took on the night fighting role. V6931 DZ-D was flown by New Zealander F/Lt 'Blackie' Smith, who painted a fern leaf motif under the standard three-stack exhausts.

Bottom right: Hurricane Mk I, P3712 ZJ•J of 96 Squadron. Apart from the overall matt black RDM2 finish, the aircraft sported a red serial number but retained Medium Sea Grey codes. P3712 was also fitted with six-stack exhaust manifolds (to reduce glare) and a 'pointed' Rotol propeller spinner.

Below: 85 Squadron chose to tone down the fuselage roundels on their night fighting Hurricanes, but kept the white squadron hexagon under the cockpit. Note the spacing of the six-stack exhausts from this angle.

Below inset: The fin flash on VY-X was also left untouched.

Soldiering on!   Left top to bottom:

Top: Mk I, V6703, HE•A joined 263 Squadron in March 1942, possibly as a unit hack. It is seen here next to a Curtiss Commando and a 264 Squadron Defiant. V6703 was later transferred to 257 Squadron, and eventually struck off charge in January 1945.

Middle: Gloster-built Hurricane Mk I, W9132 HP•P of 247 Squadron photographed in early 1941 before the unit's codes were change to ZY (see later). W9132 was later transferred to the Middle East and served with 30 Squadron from June to September 1941, when it force-landed on Idku Lake, Nile Delta, Egypt.

Bottom and right: Gloster-built Hurricane Mk I, W9200 DX•? of 245 Squadron in early May 1941. This aircraft was flown by the unit's CO, Squadron Leader John Simpson DFC, (sitting in the cockpit) when the unit was based at Aldergrove, Co Antrim, Northern Ireland. The cartoon is of a jester within a (yellow) diamond. There are eleven swastika 'kill' marks under the cockpit sill, the last of which was claimed on 8th April 1941. The 'invisible' yellow surround to the fuselage roundel was caused by the orthochromatic film used.

ENTER THE Mk II

Comparison views of the main differences between the Merlin III-engined Mk I and the Merlin XX-engined Mk II.

Left: The Mk I can be identified by the short wing root fairing (arrowed) on the cowling side.

Below: The nose cowling of the Mk II was 4.5 inches longer that the Mk I, measured from the panel line (A) in front of the windscreen to the panel line (B) immediately to the rear of the exhaust manifolds. This caused the wing root fairing on the cowling side to be elongated. The carburettor intake (C) was also moved, being positioned a few inches further back on the Mk II (see page 21). The difference in cowling fasteners (D) is shown on page 3.

Upper right: The Mk I's underside radiator bath had a shallow oval-shaped intake and vertically ribbed radiator and oil cooler.

Lower right: The Mk II's radiator was deeper and had a more rectangular-shaped intake with a circular oil cooler in the centre.

Inset left: Z2346 was built by Hawkers and completed in the summer of 1940. The early aircraft were fitted with 'pointed' Rotol propeller spinners and factory-applied Sky under surfaces. Z2346 was retained by Hawkers and used by Rolls-Royce for trials, not being struck off charge until July 1944.

Main image: An early Mk IIa, Z2334 saw operational RAF service with 605, 242 and 605 Squadron before being sent to Russia in early 1942. It has the usual 'pointed' Rotol propeller spinner and factory-applied Sky under surfaces. Both aircraft on this page were fitted with TR9B radios indicated by the triangular 'tab' on the aerial mast and the short mast on top of the rudder. The Mk IIa retained the same eight-gun armament of the Mk I. The ring mounted behind the spinner on many Mk IIs was to prevent oil, shed by the constant speed mechanism, being blown onto the windshield.

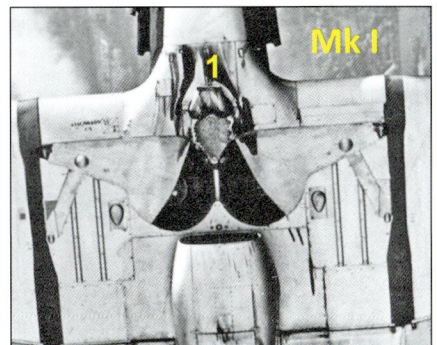

Left: The Mk I had a distinctive 'W' shaped carburettor intake (1) whereas the Mk II had a much longer intake (2) that extended back into the panel between the wheel wells.

Main photo: This badly censored print of Hurricane Mk IIa Z2451 shows some interesting details such as the fin and rudder stencilling (A), the supercharger volute drain tube (B) in the ventral fillet (see page 33), the starboard formation lamp cover (C) and the internal struts for the larger radiator (D). The Mk II also introduced a much needed ability to control the rudder trim tab (E) from the cockpit. The way the upper camouflage has been painted down over the ventral fillet just in front of the rudder is very unusual.

The rudder stencil reads Z2451 41H/151598 CX. The 41H is the Air Ministry code for Hawker aircraft and CX refers to the Cellon dope applied to the fabric on the rudder.

Right: Z2770, NN•J of 310 (Czech) Squadron, an eight-gun Mk IIa, at the Duxford firing butts in the summer of 1941. The formation-keeping lamp window is visible on the first N (arrowed). Z2770 was sent to Russia in January 1942.

Below: Z2487 was also an eight-gun Mk IIa. It had a longer life, serving with two front-line squadrons, 306 and 32. It then went to the Station Flight at Northolt, in whose codes, FC•T, it was photographed in mid-1941. Later, it served with 9 Pilots Advance Flying Unit (PAFU) and 59 and 56 OTUs before being struck off charge in July 1944. Again, there is an oil collector ring behind the spinner. This ring only covered the upper two thirds of the spinner.

Note that on both aircraft, the lower foot step stirrup (A) has been pulled down, so the upper hand hold cover (B) has automatically opened. When the pilot had climbed onto the wing, he pushed the hand hold cover flush, and the foot step was pulled back up by a connected internal bungee cord. A feature often missed in model kits.

IMPROVING FIRE-POWER, THE Mk IIb

Hurricane Mk IIb, Z3661, photographed at Hunsdon on 6 September 1941. This was a twelve-gun machine, note how the outer two gun barrels are staggered and protrude from the wing leading edge. The two intakes/vents on the cowling side (A) are for cooling the generator. The circular hole (B) is for the inertia starting handle and appeared on both port and starboard sides of the cowling. Z3661 served with 3 Squadron until mid-1941.

Hurricane Mk IIb production began in February 1941, and most were fitted with 'pointed' Rotol CM/1 spinners.

Right: A camouflaged Mk IIb wing with the two outer machine gun loading panels removed.

Below: An unpainted Mk IIb wing at the factory with all gun panels removed. The outer guns were aligned together horizontally with the main spar but the outer gun was mounted slightly lower than the inner gun. The four main guns (A,B,C,D) were stepped forwards and backwards to allow the belt feeds (E) to be fitted alongside each other.

Above:: Trials of the 12 gun armament began in June/July 1940 but production didn't begin until February 1941. This is a Mk IIb in mid-1940 colours.

Below: Head-on view of a Mk IIb showing the positions of the outer two machine guns in relation to the landing lights and inner four machine guns. Note the shape of the 'pointed' wooden Jablo blades and wear on the leading edge of the metal sheathing.

Left: An armourer loading the outer machine guns of Z3661 seen on p23. The Mk IIb was normally armed with around 4,000 rounds of .303 inch ammunition for its twelve machine guns, which was reduced when bomb racks were fitted (see p34). The 'stepped' main guns can clearly be seen in this view.

Below: An NV coded 79 Squadron Mk IIb, photographed at either Pembrey or Fairwood Common in Wales. The aircraft is probably finished in the Mixed Grey/Dark Green upper surfaces with Medium Sea Grey under surfaces Day Fighter Scheme, with yellow outer wing leading edges and a (truncated) rear fuselage band. It is fitted with 'fishtail' exhausts and a a Rotol CM/1 spinner.

79 Squadron was sent to Wales for a rest following its involvement in the Battle of Britain. It was tasked with patrolling the Irish Sea and Liverpool area – hence the fitting of the 44 gallon long-range tanks. It stayed in Wales until March 1942, when the squadron sailed for India.

Above: Hurricane Mk IIb, BD728, FN•T of 331 (Norwegian) Squadron, photographed in the late summer of 1941. It is finished in the newly introduced grey/green Day Fighter Scheme, with prominent yellow wing leading edges, freshly-painted Sky spinner and rear fuselage band. The serial number is forward of its usual position over the individual aircraft letter.

Above right: 2nd Lt Jens Müller standing in front of his Mk IIb, BD734, FN•D, named 'Odin' at Skeabrae in September 1941. The shield on the cowling side was copied from the school pin of Lt Müller's girlfriend, Alice Taylor, who he met while training in Canada.

Right: Starboard-side view of BD734 FN•D. The Norwegian national flag appeared on both sides below the cockpit, as did the name 'Odin' partially hidden in this view by the shadow cast by the propeller blade. The Sky rear fuselage band does not cover the serial number that covers the 'F' of the code letter. The spinner is a 'bullet-shaped' Rotol ES/9, identified by the locking studs (arrowed) between the blades.

331 was the first of the Norwegian fighter squadrons to form in the RAF and was based at Castletown, Caithness, to work up on the Hurricane. It became operational in September 1941 and moved to Skeabrae, Orkney, providing defence for northern Scotland.

Above: Intimate view of two airframe fitters working on the interior of a 401 Squadron Mk IIb at Digby on 24th July 1941. The port fabric panel has been removed, revealing the radio box (arrowed). The stencil above the panel reads '? IS REAR OXYGEN CYLINDER TURNED ON'. A clear vision 'knock-out' panel is in the port front bottom corner of the canopy hood.

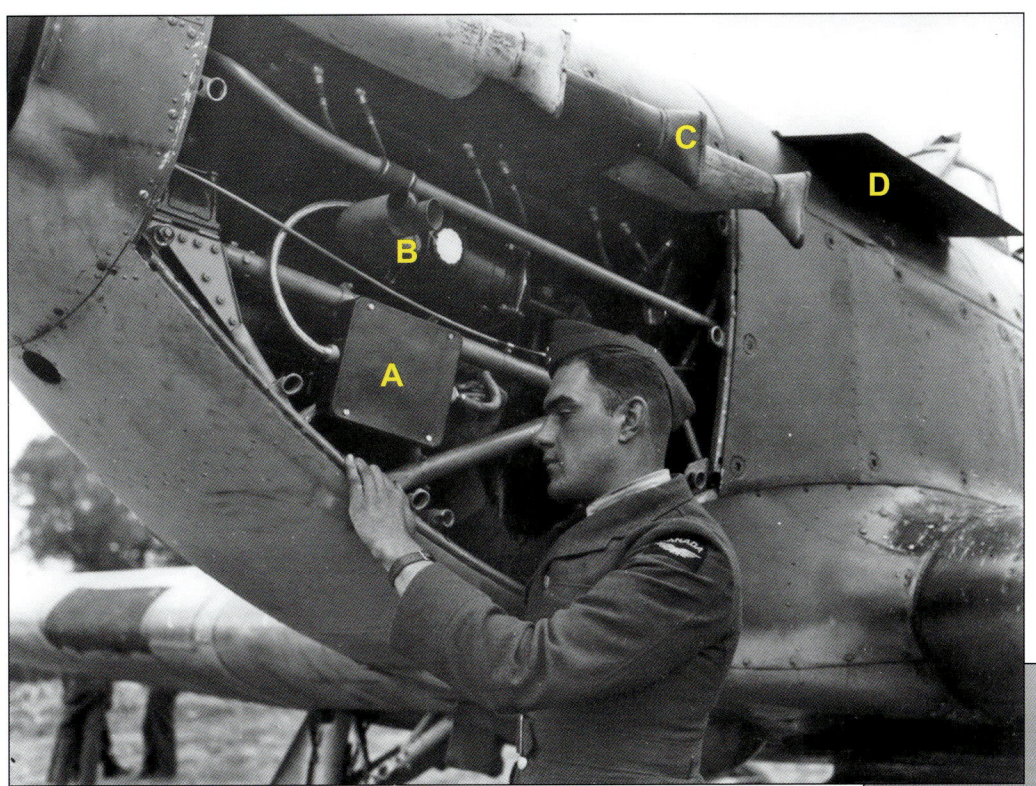

More photos from the sequence taken at Digby in July 1941.

Above: LAC E Fairwell looking into the engine cowling of a 401 Squadron Mk IIb. The 'black box' (A) is the ignition control unit suppressor to stop electrical interference with the radio. The two intakes/vents (B) are for generator cooling. It has 'fishtail' exhausts (C) and the anti-glare shield (D) for night flying.

Above right: Testing the TR1133 VHF radio. Most of the engine cowling panels have been removed, revealing the 28 gallon reserve fuel tank in front of the windscreen (E). The circular object (F) is the filler cap for the 7 gallon oil tank fitted in the port wing leading edge.

Right: An unusual view of a Hurricane with the cockpit emergency exit panel removed. Unlike the Spitfire, the Hurricane didn't have a hinged 'cockpit door'. Instead, it had this panel on the starboard side that could be jettisoned by sliding the hood all the way back and then pulling a handle in the door. Here it has been removed, presumably to allow ground-crew more elbow room, or to give the photographer a better view!

A formation of six 601 Squadron Hurricane Mk IIbs (thought to be B Flight) photographed during the late summer of 1941. The squadron was engaged on Channel Sweeps and escorts out of Manston, prior to being (briefly) re-equipped with Bell Airacobras. They are finished in the Day Fighter Scheme with yellow outer wing leading edges. The squadron's red 'winged sword' appears in the central white stripe of the fin flash on Z3356 UF•O. Other identifiable airframes include BD711 UF•Y, Z3159 UF•W and Z3244 UF•P. UF•N appears to be an older aircraft with a full fin flash and the Sky band applied around the serial number.

HURRICANE Mk IIB, Z3356 UF•O, 601 SQUADRON, SUMMER 1941

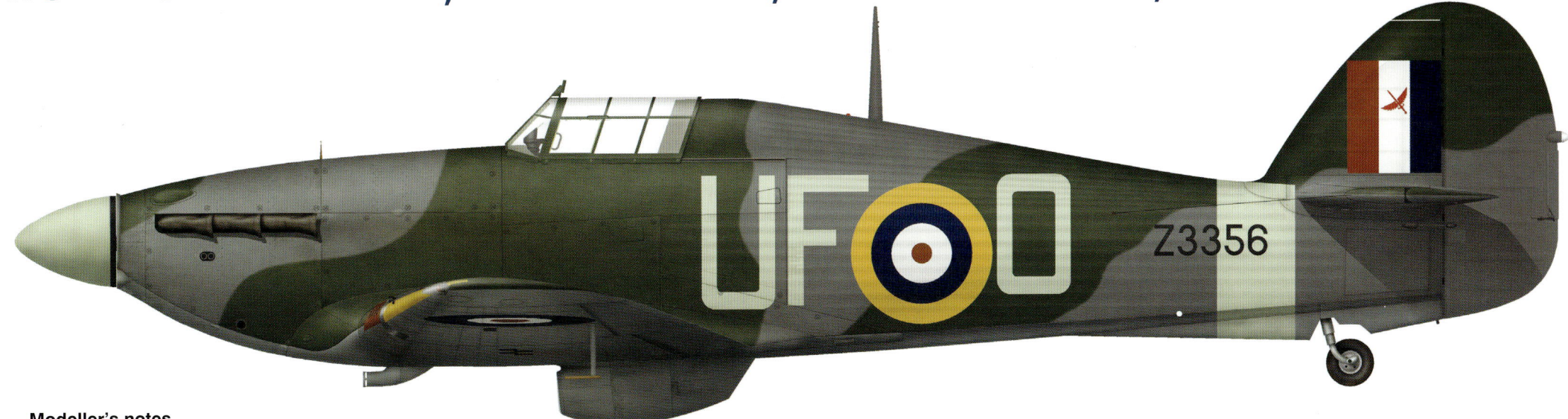

Modeller's notes

- Dark Green and Mixed Grey upper surfaces to the A Scheme pattern, with Medium Sea Grey under surfaces.
- Yellow outer wing leading edges from landing lights to navigation lights.
- Standard 8 inch high Night (black) serial number on the rear fuselage.
- Sky spinner (with black back plate), Sky rear fuselage band and Sky codes.
- Red 601 Squadron 'winged sword' on the white of the fin flash.

Discussion points

- Z3356 was fitted with a bullet-shaped Rotol ES/9 'pointed' propeller spinner and wood 'Jablo' propeller blades.
- Fishtail exhaust manifolds.
- Dowty oil-spring oleo 'straight' leg tailwheel.
- Note how far to the rear the Sky fuselage band is, causing it to be truncated around leading edge of the fin.

HURRI-BOMBER

Hurricane Mk IIb, BE485, AE•W of 402 Squadron. The two 250lb bombs are attached to standard RAF Universal Bomb Carriers within shaped fairings. These were fitted under the second inboard cartridge case ejection chutes, resulting in those guns being removed. The two outer machine guns' ejection chutes are arrowed.

On this aircraft the leading edge yellow stripe has been extended beyond the navigation light to the wing-tip.

Inset: The Hurri-bombers all benefited from the newly introduced Dowty oleo-pneumatic 'knuckled' leg tailwheel.

Opposite page: Hurricane Mk IIb, BN114, while serving with the A&AEE in early 1942. The bomb carriers are loaded with 500lb GP bombs. In the upper view the flaps are deployed showing the internal strengthening ribs. In the lower view it can be seen that the aircraft is fitted with an ES/9 propeller spinner, identified by the six locking studs (A) and wooden Jablo propeller blades with metal sheathing on the leading edges. The twelve machine gun ports have been taped over with red dope patches. It has the 'old' TR9 radio wire attachments. The small pipe (B) under the ventral fairing is the supercharger volute drain tube that was introduced on the Mk II. It appears on most Mk IIs in this position.

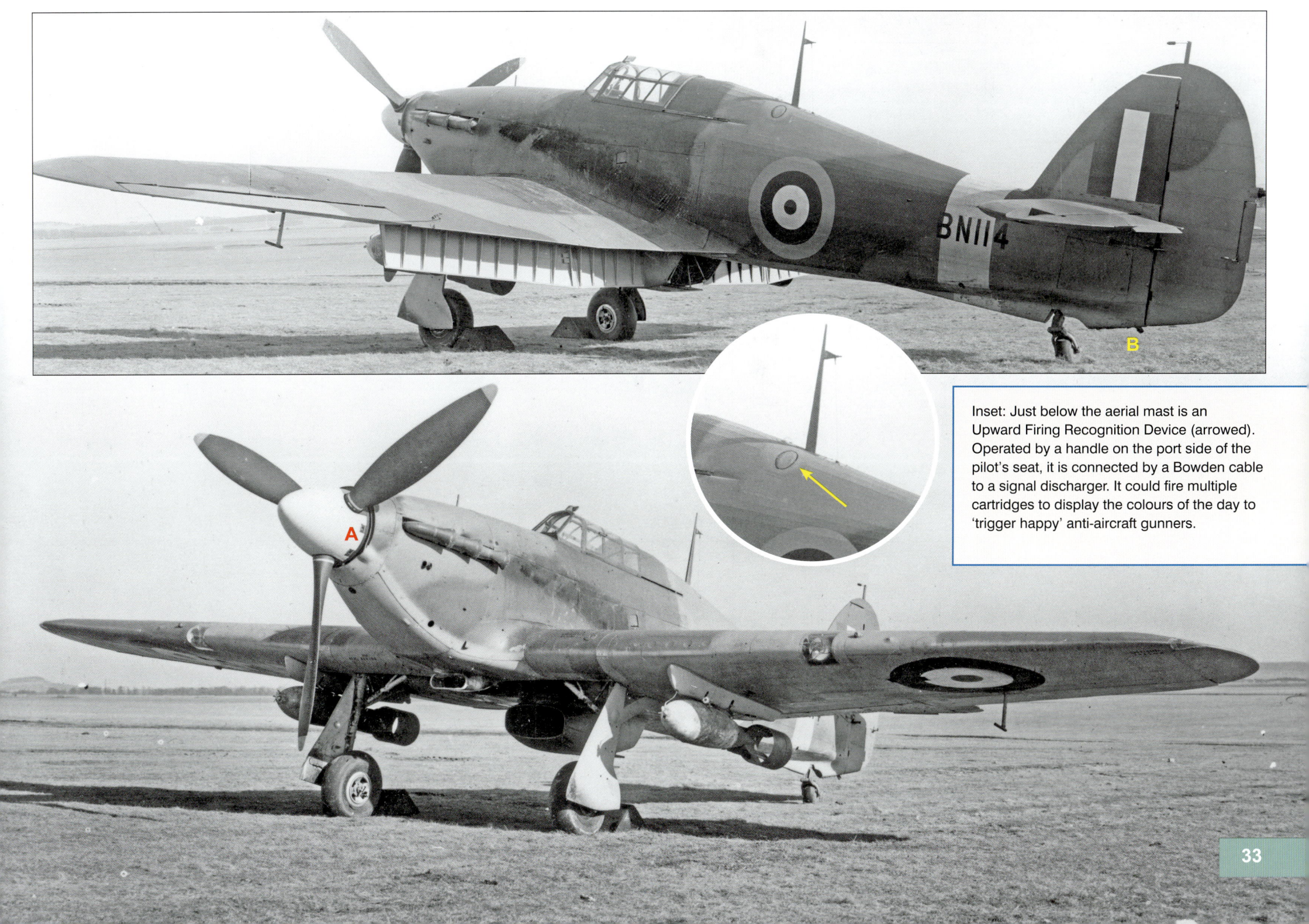

Inset: Just below the aerial mast is an Upward Firing Recognition Device (arrowed). Operated by a handle on the port side of the pilot's seat, it is connected by a Bowden cable to a signal discharger. It could fire multiple cartridges to display the colours of the day to 'trigger happy' anti-aircraft gunners.

402 Squadron armourers pose for the camera loading a 250lb GP bomb on AE•S (possibly BE477) while the pilot looks on. 402 became the first 'Hurri-bomber' unit, starting operations in this role in November 1941.
As the 'second' ejection chute was covered by the bomb carrier fairing, the airflow was interrupted, causing air pressure in the gun bay to increase. The gun port was therefore blanked off (A). Later some a/c had under-wing vents fitted to prevent pressure build up.
(B) is a gun camera fairing (either a G.42B or a G.45 camera).

Corporals Graham and Ryland RCAF, standing in front of AE•Q, thought to be BE489, 402 Squadron's CO, Squadron/Ldr Robert Morrow's aircraft, beneath the 'Butch the Falcon' illustration on the port cowling panel, at Warmwell in late1941/early 1942. Note that the propeller spinner appears to have been removed. The hole behind their heads (arrowed) is the attachment point for the hand crank, retained despite the Mk II having electrical engine starting.

Two photos of Squadron Leader Morrow, straddling the cockpit of a 402 Squadron Mk IIb, being loaded with 250lb bombs in early 1942.

The hard-edged demarcation between the two upper surface camouflage colours on the engine cowling looks to be brush painted. Unusually for the time, this aircraft has the early style exhausts.

The bomb trolley in the foreground is a standard 4-wheel steerable Type C, able to carry up to 4,000lb loads.

Main image: A 402 Squadron Hurricane Mk IIb in a sandbag-lined dispersal bay at Warmwell in early 1942. Its individual aircraft letter appears to be 'A' (see under the nose and the tip of the letter just visible above the wing near the landing light). Again, there is a hard demarcation between the upper surface Mixed Grey and Dark Green camouflage colours and the upper/under surface colours. It is difficult to differentiate between the 'light' Mixed Grey and the under surface Medium Sea Grey.

Inset: The similarly camouflaged Mk IIb, coded AE•D. This aircraft may be the replacement for the earlier 'D' BE483, which was shot down by Me 109s off Cherbourg on 2 January 1942 (see pages 38 and 39).

The 'original' AE•D, BE483, on its nose in late 1941. The Sky band encircles the whole fuselage. It has a Dowty oleo-pneumatic 'knuckled' tail-wheel leg. BE483 was shot down by Me 109s off Cherbourg on 2nd January 1942 with its pilot, F/Sgt B P O'Neill RCAF. The extreme staining under the aircraft's centre section may be linked to the crash landing.

HURRICANE Mk IIB, BE483 AE•D, 402 SQUADRON, AUTUMN 1941

Modeller's notes

- Dark Green and Mixed Grey upper surfaces to the A Scheme pattern, with Medium Sea Grey under surfaces.
- Yellow outer wing leading edges from landing lights to navigation lights.
- Standard 8 inch high Night (black) serial number on the rear fuselage.
- Sky spinner (with black back plate) Sky rear fuselage band and Sky codes.
- Black individual aircraft letter 'D' under nose.

Discussion points

- Fitted with anti-glare shields
- Gun camera fairing on starboard wing leading edge
- Dowty oleo-pneumatic 'knuckled' tail-wheel leg.
- Under-wing No1 Universal Bomb Carrier in a fairing fitted under the second inboard cartridge case ejection chute.

Left: Sgt Scott of 402 Squadron (RCAF) giving the 'V for Victory' sign in front of a 250lb bomb which has the words 'We Always Deliver' chalked on the fin cone ring.

Right: 402 Squadron Mk IIb Z5054 coded AE•Q, circa September 1941. Z5054 shows that the Mixed Grey paint has been applied by brush, leaving streaky patches and hard demarcation lines with the original Dark Green paint.

The pilots are Sgt Graham David 'Robbie' Robertson, RCAF (wearing the flying helmet) and the 'line shooter' (possibly Sgt Handley). The latter has his microphone lead hooked onto the IFF aerial wire (arrowed).

Hurricane Mk IIb, coded HH•T of 175 Squadron, dispersed in trees at Warmwell in the early spring of 1942. The accumulator trolley appears to be of the type fitted with a small engine on the top.

Below: 174 (Mauritius) Squadron Mk IIbs at Manston, circa May 1942. BE684 XP•Y and BE421 XP•G are in the foreground. Both aircraft had previously served with 607 Squadron before being allocated to 174 and both were 'lost to enemy action' in the summer of 1942. BE421 was shot down over the Forest D'Eu in June, Sgt C R Mort RAF becoming a PoW. BE684 was lost attacking Fort Rouge, Sgt W Y Dennison, RCAF, made a forced-landing west of St Omer, and also became a PoW.

Right: BE492 of 402 Squadron demonstrating a low level attack for the Press. The Hurri-bomber proved to be quite effective on low-level raids over France, although the bomb load was never enough to cause real damage to larger installations.

Hurricane Mk IIb, BE682, XP•R 'Mauritius VII' of 174 (Mauritius) Squadron, being armed with 250lb GP bombs at Manston in the early summer of 1942. This was shortly after the change in national markings as shown by the fuselage roundel and fin flash of the aircraft behind, BE684 XP•Y. Looking on are two sergeant pilots, the second from left being F/Sgt James Himiona Wetere (RNZAF), a Maori. The aircraft is fitted with a Rotol ES/9 propeller spinner, 'fishtail' exhausts, and anti-glare shields. The name 'Mauritius VII' was written in yellow stencil-style capital letters.

HURRICANE Mk.IIc

Inset top: Hurricane Mk IIc, Z3888, armed with four 20mm Hispano Mk I cannons undergoing trials at the A&AEE in the autumn of 1941. In November 1943, Z3888 was shipped to India, being struck off charge in August 1945.

Main image: Front view of an early production 20mm cannon-armed Hurricane Mk IIc. Note the width of the oval 'mouth' of the carburettor intake.

Both aircraft are fitted with Mk I Hispano barrels with 'flat' recoil springs at the breech end on the barrel.

Right: The later Mk II Hispano cannon had round recoil springs further up the barrel.

Close up of a Hurricane Mk IIc's Hispano Mk I 20mm cannon barrels, showing to good effect the 'flat' recoil springs. The cannons were belt-fed, the drums on the wing being the Chatellerault mechanism used to the feed the 20mm shells in to the breech, resulting in the upper surface of the wings needing to have clearance blisters. The Hispano Mk I had 60 rounds per gun. (A) is the taped-over gun camera fairing.

Right: Armourers loading a belt of 20mm shells in to the wing of a Mk IIc. The aircraft is fitted with a Rotol CM/1 spinner.

Below: Closer view of an armourer loading a belt of cannon shells into the wing of a well used Mk IIc, judging by the wear on the surrounding wing surface. The two Chatellerault drums are resting on the access panels, showing why they had to have clearance blisters.

The first Hurricane to fly with the four-cannon wing armament was V7360. It was a Gloster-built machine, still powered by the Merlin III, which was initially allocated to 151 Squadron. F/Lt Roddick Lee 'Dick' Smith (a champion of the cannon-armed Hurricane idea) was convinced that cannon-armed fighters were the way forward and persevered with trials. He flew both L1750 (an early, externally-mounted two-cannon version) and V7360 in combat during the Battle of Britain, claiming an Me 109E 'destroyed' on 23rd August and a 'probable' on 31st August while flying V7360.

V7360 was followed by two more Merlin III-engined Mk Is (possibly V7380 and W9314) before the remainder of the cannon-armed wings were fitted to Merlin XX-powered Mk II airframes. The Mk IIc first flew in February 1941.

Another view of the 20mm Mk I Hispano cannon barrels with 'flat' recoil springs. Also noticeable in this photo are the light coloured 'fishtail' exhausts (painted in glare-reducing high temperature paint) and the hole for the hand crank starter.

Above: Close-up of Hurricane Mk IIc, BD948 QO•X of 3 Squadron in the grey and green Day Fighter Scheme introduced in August 1941. The aircraft is fitted with a Rotol CM/1 propeller spinner, with a black painted back plate, Mk I Hispano 20mm cannons, anti-glare shield, a 'knuckled' tail-wheel leg with modified ventral fairing and a cowling-top bead sight. The supercharger drain tube (arrowed) is further forward than usual on this aircraft.

Right: Hurricane Mk IIc, BD867, QO•Y of 3 Squadron. It was delivered from 44 MU on 12th August 1941. The squadron was based at Stapleford Tawney, Essex, from the summer of 1941 until the summer of 1942.

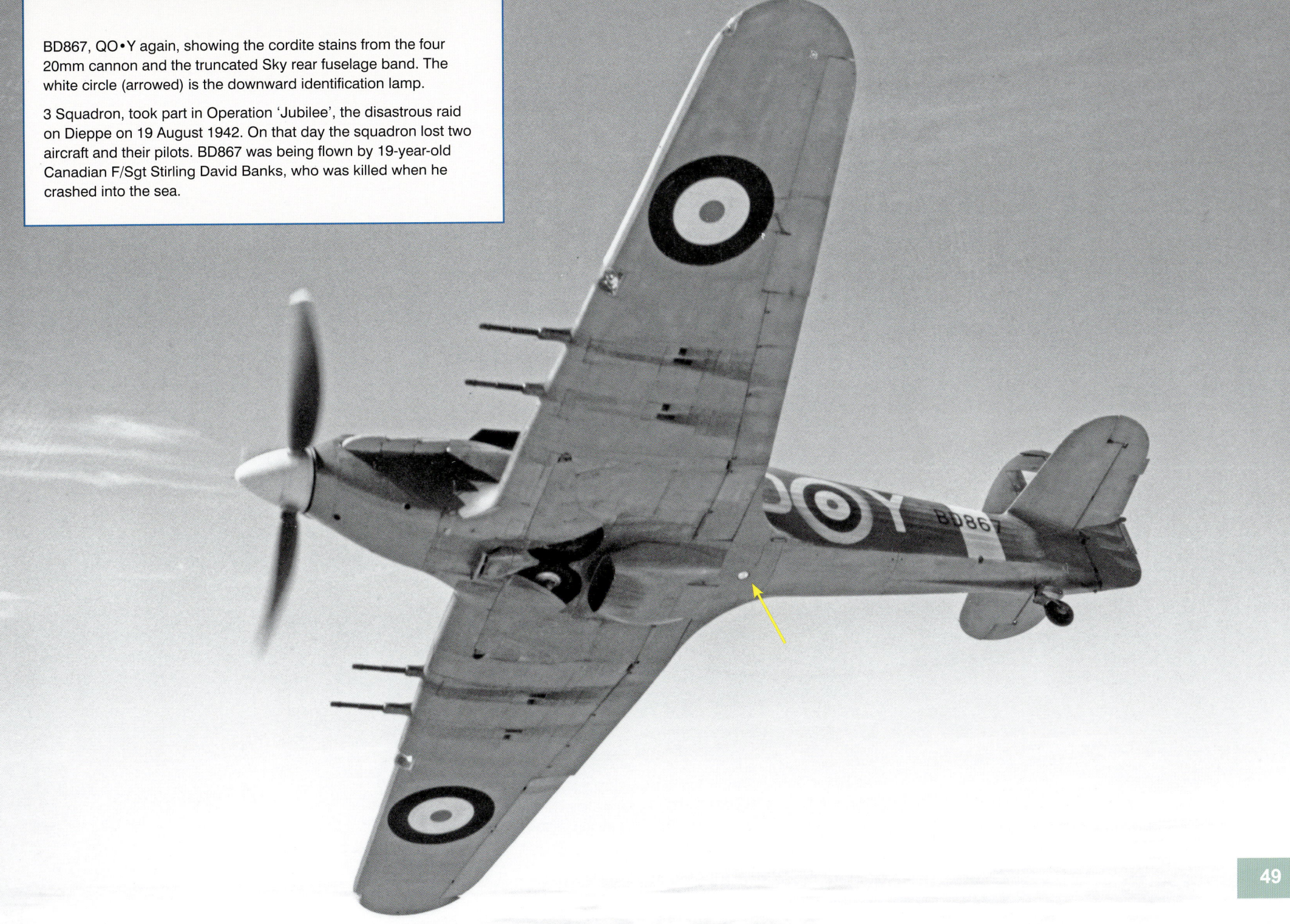

BD867, QO•Y again, showing the cordite stains from the four 20mm cannon and the truncated Sky rear fuselage band. The white circle (arrowed) is the downward identification lamp.

3 Squadron, took part in Operation 'Jubilee', the disastrous raid on Dieppe on 19 August 1942. On that day the squadron lost two aircraft and their pilots. BD867 was being flown by 19-year-old Canadian F/Sgt Stirling David Banks, who was killed when he crashed into the sea.

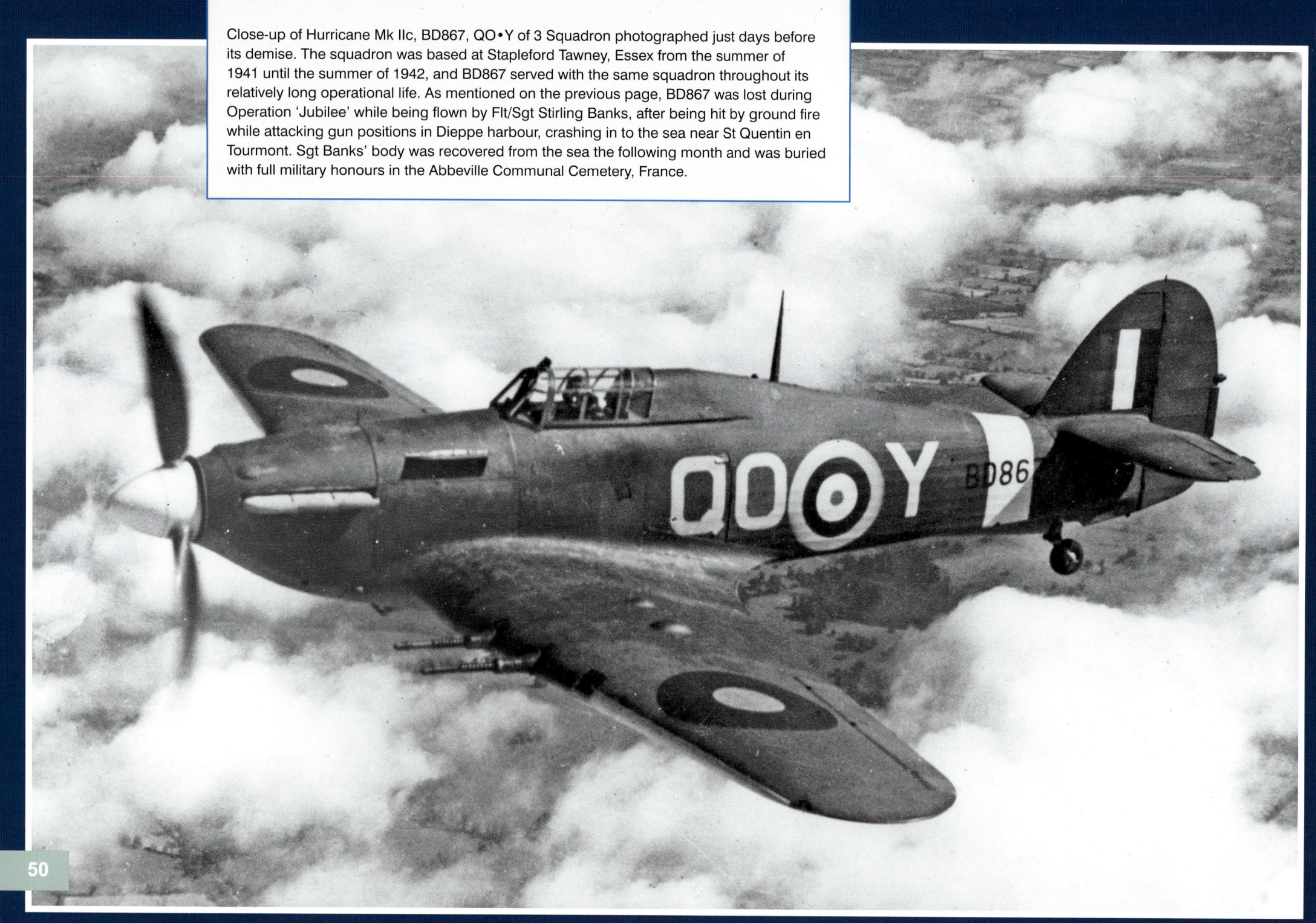

Close-up of Hurricane Mk IIc, BD867, QO•Y of 3 Squadron photographed just days before its demise. The squadron was based at Stapleford Tawney, Essex from the summer of 1941 until the summer of 1942, and BD867 served with the same squadron throughout its relatively long operational life. As mentioned on the previous page, BD867 was lost during Operation 'Jubilee' while being flown by Flt/Sgt Stirling Banks, after being hit by ground fire while attacking gun positions in Dieppe harbour, crashing in to the sea near St Quentin en Tourmont. Sgt Banks' body was recovered from the sea the following month and was buried with full military honours in the Abbeville Communal Cemetery, France.

HURRICANE Mk IIC BD867 QO•Y, 3 SQUADRON, SUMMER 1942

Modeller's notes

- Dark Green and Mixed Grey upper surfaces to the A Scheme pattern, with Medium Sea Grey under surfaces (Day Fighter Scheme).
- Yellow outer wing leading edges from landing lights to navigation lights.
- Standard 8 inch high Night (black) serial number on the rear fuselage.
- Sky spinner, rear fuselage band and codes.

Discussion points

- 'Pointed' Rotol CM/1 propeller spinner and wooden 'Jablo' propeller blades.
- Armed with four Mk I Hispano 20mm cannon with 'flat' recoil springs.
- Early style exhaust manifolds.
- Anti-glare shields.
- Dowty oleo-pneumatic 'knuckled' leg tailwheel.
- Note how the Sky rear fuselage band is truncated along the upper/under surface demarcation line.

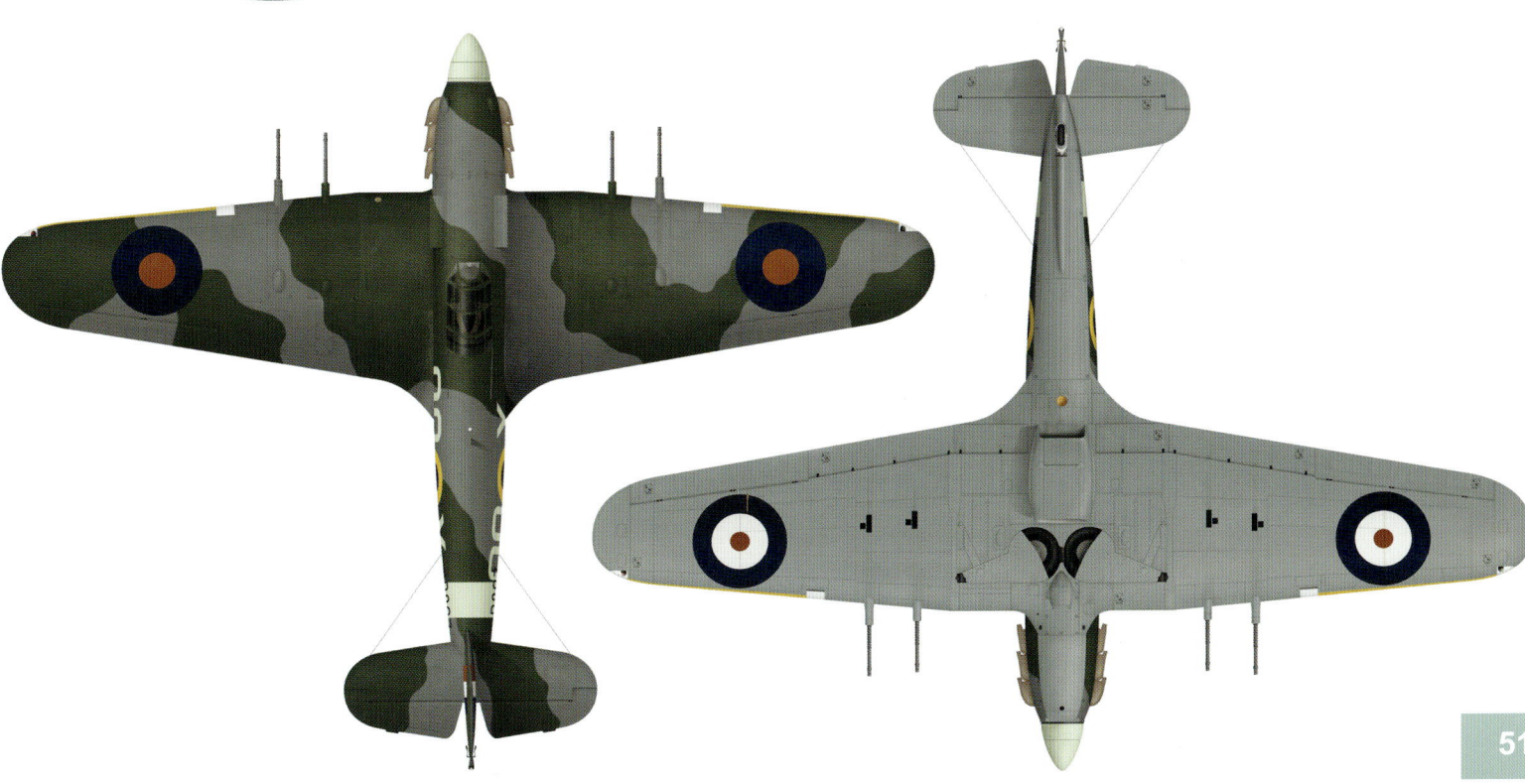

Left: Mk IIc, Z2891, QO•K of 3 Squadron, about to land. The aircraft is fitted with the older 'straight' tail-wheel referred to as the 'Dowty Spring Type', and 'fishtail' exhausts. Z2891 had previously served with AFDU and later with 615 and 32 Squadrons before being sent to Russia in June 1942.

Main image: Another view of BD867, QO•Y showing to good effect its Rotol CM/1 propeller spinner identified by the single slot on the backing plate.

This and the following page: Contemporary formation shots of 3 Squadron Hurricane Mk IIcs, taken during a Press photo flight in the summer of 1941. The left hand photo shows Z3464 QO•Z, nearest the camera, BD868 QO•P, BD867 QO•Y, Z3068 QO•F, Z3092 QO•T and Z3894 QO•R.

In the right hand photo the formation has changed to show Z3068 QO•F nearest the camera with Z3092 QO•T, Z3894 QO•R, BD868 QO•P, Z3464 QO•Z and BD867 QO•Y.

The BD series aircraft have the later 'knuckled' tail-wheel. QO•Y is the only one to be fitted with an exhaust glare shields, which were easily removable.

Main image: Our camera plane has changed position again. Z3464 QO•Z, BD868 QO•P, BD867 QO•Y, Z3068 QO•F, Z3092 QO•T, Z3894 QO•R.

Of the six aircraft in these photographs, three were lost to enemy action (along with their pilots). Z3464 in October 1941 with 615 Squadron. BD867 on 19th August 1942. BD868 on 7th June 1942. Z3068 was lost in a flying accident in April 1942 while serving with 43 Squadron. Z3894 was sent to Russia in January 1943. Z3092 was transferred to India and struck off charge in November 1944.

Right: Another view of Mk IIc Z3888, (see p44), this time fitted with 44 gallon long-range tanks. The tanks were non-jettisonable and combat stressed to 4g. This view shows the A Scheme camouflage pattern to good effect.

Below: Originally built as an eight-gun Mk IIa, Z2905 was returned to Hawkers following a brief spell serving with 1 Squadron in the spring of 1941. It had cannon-armed wings fitted, before being allocated to the A&AEE, where it was photographed in February 1942, fitted with 90 gallon non-jettisonable ferry tanks. The inscription just to the rear of the canopy hood reads 'McConnell's Squadron No 34', identifying Z2905 as one of 45 presentation aircraft sponsored by Canadian sugar refiner, newspaper publisher and philanthropist, John Wilson McConnell, who donated $1 million for the 'Wings for Britain' campaign.

Note the eyebolts under the wingtips (arrowed) for 'picketing'.

NIGHT FIGHTERS

Main image: As featured on the first page in colour, 87 Squadron Mk IIc, BE500 LK•A, flown by Squadron Leader Denis Smallwood, while based at Charmy Down, Somerset in early 1942. The aircraft is finished in the Night Fighter Scheme of overall RDM2 Special Night. Note the Squadron Leader's pennant under the windscreen. BE500, carried the name 'Cawnpore I' written in white underneath a green scroll containing the words 'United Provinces'. It was one of the many presentation aircraft gifted from Britain's colonies, and one of at least seventeen Hurricanes from the 'United Provinces' fund of India.

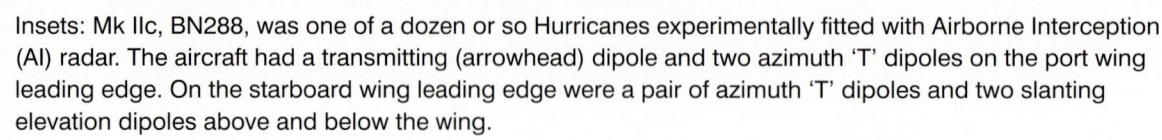

Insets: Mk IIc, BN288, was one of a dozen or so Hurricanes experimentally fitted with Airborne Interception (AI) radar. The aircraft had a transmitting (arrowhead) dipole and two azimuth 'T' dipoles on the port wing leading edge. On the starboard wing leading edge were a pair of azimuth 'T' dipoles and two slanting elevation dipoles above and below the wing.

Squadron Leader Smallwood, in BE500 LK•A, leading a section of 87 Squadron Hurricane Mk IIcs circa May 1942. Identifiable airframes include LK•B Z3775, LK•G BD952 and LK•F BE512 (or BE513). All the aircraft have Medium Sea Grey code letters and red serial numbers. Only the Z Series Hurricane LK•B has the old style tailwheel.

All the Hurricanes carry the scroll 'United Provinces' under the cockpit with an individual Indian province name underneath. The two insets show 'Bahraich' and 'Agra', the latter being the location of the Taj Mahal.

Right: Other Hurricane squadrons involved in the night fighting role included 151 Squadron, represented here by Mk IIc, Z3440, finished in a well-weathered overall RDM2 Special Night finish. The squadron converted to the night fighting role in November 1940. It was initially equipped with Boulton Paul Defiants, which it operated alongside Hurricane Mk Is for a few months, before receiving Hurricane Mk IIcs in April 1941. It kept both types until fully re-equipped with Mosquito NF IIs in April 1942.

Main image: Soon to become a celebrated airframe in the hands of the legendary F/Lt Karel Miroslav Kuttelwascher, 1 Squadron Mk IIc, BE581 JX•E was photographed before the changeover of national markings in May/June 1942. This was before the application of the 'Night Reaper' scroll and scythe on the nose, or the grey/green Intruder Scheme. It still has Medium Sea Grey codes. The front of the ES/9 propeller spinner is painted red.

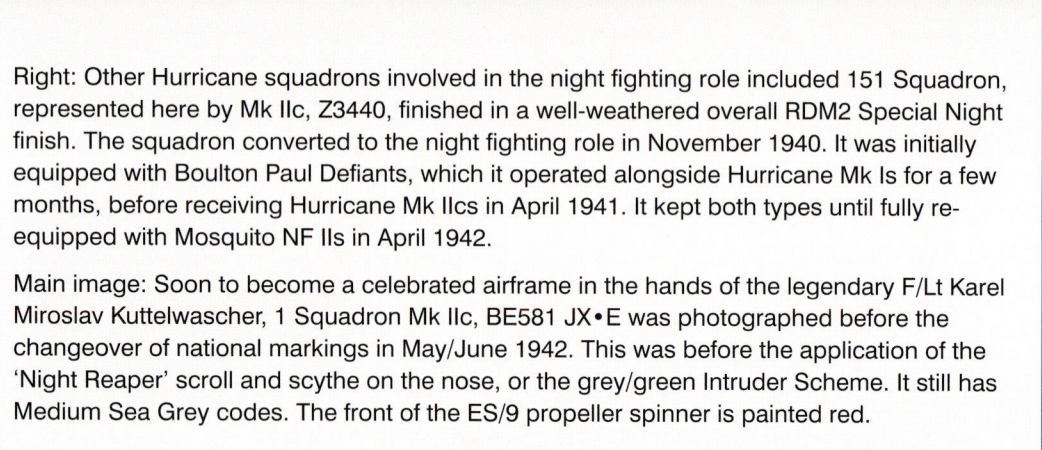

Right: The man himself, F/Lt Karel Kuttelwascher (left), crouching on the wing of BE581 – if the row of five white swastika 'kill' markings are anything to go by. The five 'kills' also date the photo to mid-April 1942 after Kuttelwascher's fifth victory, a Do 217 on the night of 16/17th April. Note the sheathed 20mm cannon barrels and the 44 gallon long-range tank. Just visible on the tank is a white oblong with red stencil that reads 'MAX LOAD 44 IMP GALS'.

Below: A Hurricane Mk IIc, thought to be Z3263, in overall RDM2 finish, with the presentation name 'Mau Molo Turi' in white under the cockpit sill, gifted by several Kenyan tribal chiefs. The aircraft is listed as a Mk IIb, but has the Chatellerault drum feed mechanism clearance blisters of a IIc. It has a small (18 inch diameter) fuselage roundel and 18 inch square fin flash.

Bottom: Sgt Brier of 43 Squadron leaning on the wing of his Hurricane Mk IIc 'Lothaire'. In this instance, the aircraft has the full size 36 inch diameter fuselage roundel and red code letters. The 'fishtail' exhaust manifolds painted in a special High Temperature Paint (HTP 41) to reduced exhaust glow at night appear particularly light.

Main image and inset: On 29th April 1942 247 Squadron took part in an air-to-air photo session with an Air Ministry photographer in a Douglas Havoc. Hurricane Mk IIc BE634 ZY•V was flown by 247's CO, Squadron Leader Peter O'Brian, DFC, a Canadian national who flew six operational sorties in the aircraft. The other aircraft is BD936 ZY•S. Note the contrast of the matt RDM2 with the sheen on the wing roundels.

This page: A closer view of BD936 ZY•S, showing the small 18 inch diameter fuselage roundel and 18 inch high red codes. The squadron and individual aircraft letters are separated by a hyphen. The serial number is smaller than usual, approximately 4 inches high.

This page: Another view of BD936 ZY•S of 247 'China British' Squadron (in recognition of the donations made by the British communities in China). It has a Rotol ES/9 spinner, 'fishtail' exhausts, anti-glare shields and Mk I Hispano 20mm cannons with flat recoil springs. Unusually for a BE Series aircraft, it has an early 'straight' Dowty Spring Type tailwheel leg.

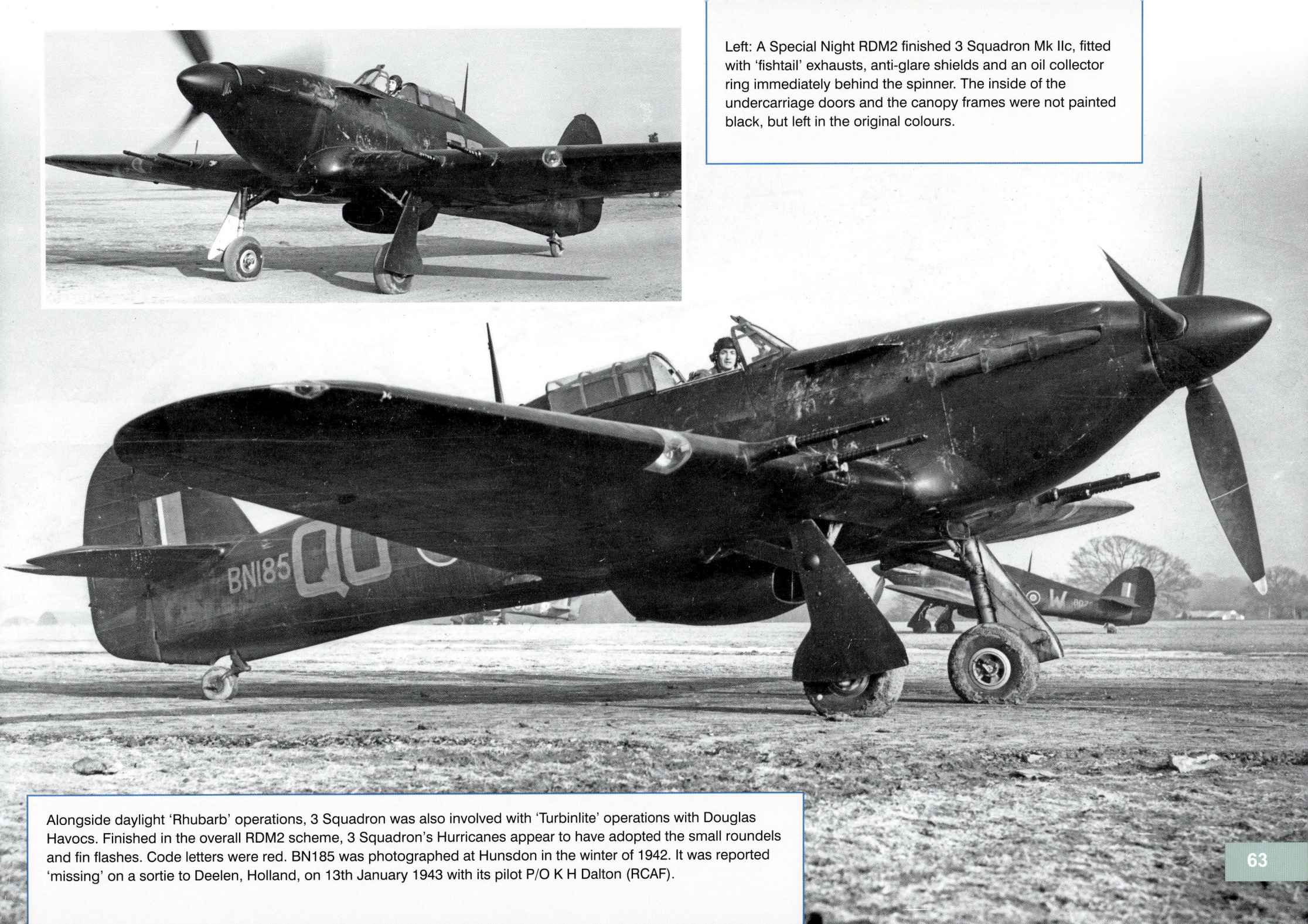

Left: A Special Night RDM2 finished 3 Squadron Mk IIc, fitted with 'fishtail' exhausts, anti-glare shields and an oil collector ring immediately behind the spinner. The inside of the undercarriage doors and the canopy frames were not painted black, but left in the original colours.

Alongside daylight 'Rhubarb' operations, 3 Squadron was also involved with 'Turbinlite' operations with Douglas Havocs. Finished in the overall RDM2 scheme, 3 Squadron's Hurricanes appear to have adopted the small roundels and fin flashes. Code letters were red. BN185 was photographed at Hunsdon in the winter of 1942. It was reported 'missing' on a sortie to Deelen, Holland, on 13th January 1943 with its pilot P/O K H Dalton (RCAF).

Main image and insets: This sequence of 87 Squadron was taken a few days after Operation 'Jubilee', 19th August 1942. A few days before 'Jubilee' the squadron's aircraft were hastily over-painted in Dark Green and Medium Sea Grey upper surfaces (in a rough approximation of the A Scheme pattern) over the original black Special Night scheme to create the Intruder Scheme. LK•A is believed to be S/Ldr Smallwood's BE500. Other aircraft in the photo include LK•T (a Mk IIa), LK•Q BD833, LK•C, LK•J Z2643 (another Mk IIa) and LK•E. The serial numbers of most have been painted over.

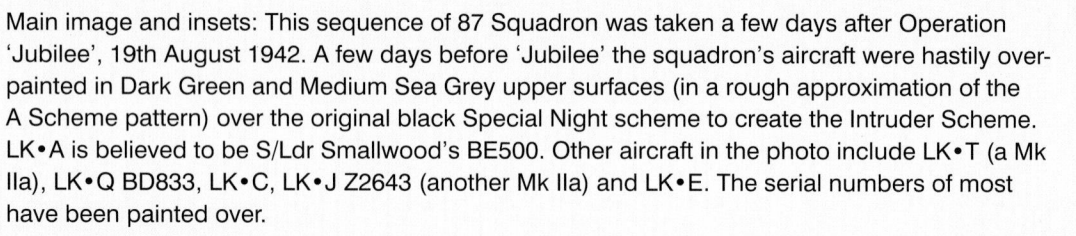

Main image and above: Photographers visited 87 at Charmy Down on 2nd September 1942. HL864 was coded LK•? and named 'Nightingale', in a scroll under the cockpit. P/O F W Mitchell is standing on the wing root.

Top left: LK•R, HL865, 'Night Duty', with Sgt B Bawden in front. HL864 LK•? is in the background.

These aircraft (and a third, HL866, named 'Night Nurse' - ex 135 Squadron) all had names with nursing connotations. They had been gifted from funds raised by Nurses of Great Britain via 'The Nursing Mirror Fighter Fund'. Both aircraft are finished in a unit-applied Intruder Scheme, with red spinners and have 44 gallon under-wing tanks. They are armed with Mk II Hispano 20mm cannons with 'round' recoil springs and have 'fishtail' exhaust manifolds painted in HTP 41 High Temperature Paint.

Close-up view of HL865 LK•R, 'Night Duty', with Sgt B Bawden. The two small vents (arrowed) were a cockpit ventilation modification intended for tropical climes.

This photo, and the ones on the previous page, show the hastily applied Operation 'Jubilee' scheme of Dark Green/Medium Sea Grey.

HURRICANE Mk IIC, HL865 LK•R, 87 SQUADRON, SEPTEMBER 1942

Modeller's notes
- Unit applied Dark Green and Medium Sea Grey upper surfaces roughly applied to the A Scheme pattern, over the original overall Special Night scheme to create the Intruder Scheme.
- Serial number (HL865) over-painted.
- Sky codes.

Discussion points
- Fitted with a 'pointed' Rotol ES/9 propeller spinner and 'round tip' Jablo propeller blades.
- Armed with four Mk II Hispano 20mm cannon with 'round' recoil springs.
- Fishtail exhaust manifolds in high temperature paint.
- Dowty oleo-pneumatic 'knuckled' leg tailwheel.
- 44 gallon long-range tanks.
- Crudely applied upper surface colours and undulating upper and under surface demarcation line.
- The two small vents below the footstep for cockpit ventilation.

Above: Another night intruder unit that returned to daylight intruder operations was 1 Squadron (see page 58). The squadron's Mk IIcs were hastily repainted in a unit-applied Day Fighter Scheme, complete with Sky band and spinner, before 1 Squadron re-equipped with Typhoons in the summer of 1942. JX•Y Z3778 shows the extensive wear and tear that occurred, even after a relatively short period. The serial number has been re-painted in small serif characters on the Sky band.

Left: Armourers loading 20mm cannon shells into a 1 Squadron Mk IIc's wing, The blistered access panels and the exhaust staining on the cowling side are notable. The small silhouettes under the cockpit show the destruction of three trains and one aircraft.

Above: 1 Squadron Mk IIcs, in the summer of 1942, including JX•Y Z3778, JX•S (??864), JX•I HL603, JX•B, JX•H BD946 (hidden behind JX•B) and JX•J.

JX•I HL603 arrived at the squadron in June 1942, and was probably delivered in a factory painted Day Fighter Scheme. The standard sized 8 inch high serial number painted over the factory-applied Sky band contrasts with the older repainted aircraft with small serials.

Right: JX•Y Z3378 again, showing the hastily-applied upper surface camouflage, this is especially noticeable on the cowling top. The cannon fairings are still in RDM2.

Below: Excellent starboard profile view of JX•Y, Z3778 (in small stencil style), in the Day Fighter Scheme applied over its previous overall RDM2/Special Night finish. Note the wing leading edge cannon fairings are still in RDM2. Z3778 was probably photographed while based at Acklington in Northumberland, prior to the squadron being re-equipped with Typhoons during the summer of 1942. Z3778 had previously served with 87 Sqn, but crashed on overshoot at Acklington 14/8/42.

Left: Another view of the worn undersides of Z3778, note the two roundels appear to be of slightly different proportions.

HURRICANE Mk IIC, Z3778 JX•Y, 1 SQUADRON, EARLY SUMMER 1942

Modeller's notes

• Unit applied Dark Green and Mixed Grey (or Ocean Grey?) upper surfaces roughly applied (by brush?) to the A Scheme pattern, with Medium Sea Grey under surfaces over the original overall Special Night scheme to create the Day Fighter Scheme.
• Sky spinner, rear fuselage band and codes.
• Serial Z3778 re-applied in approx 2 inch high stencil style in black over Sky rear fuselage band.
• Yellow outer wing leading edges from landing lights to navigation lights.

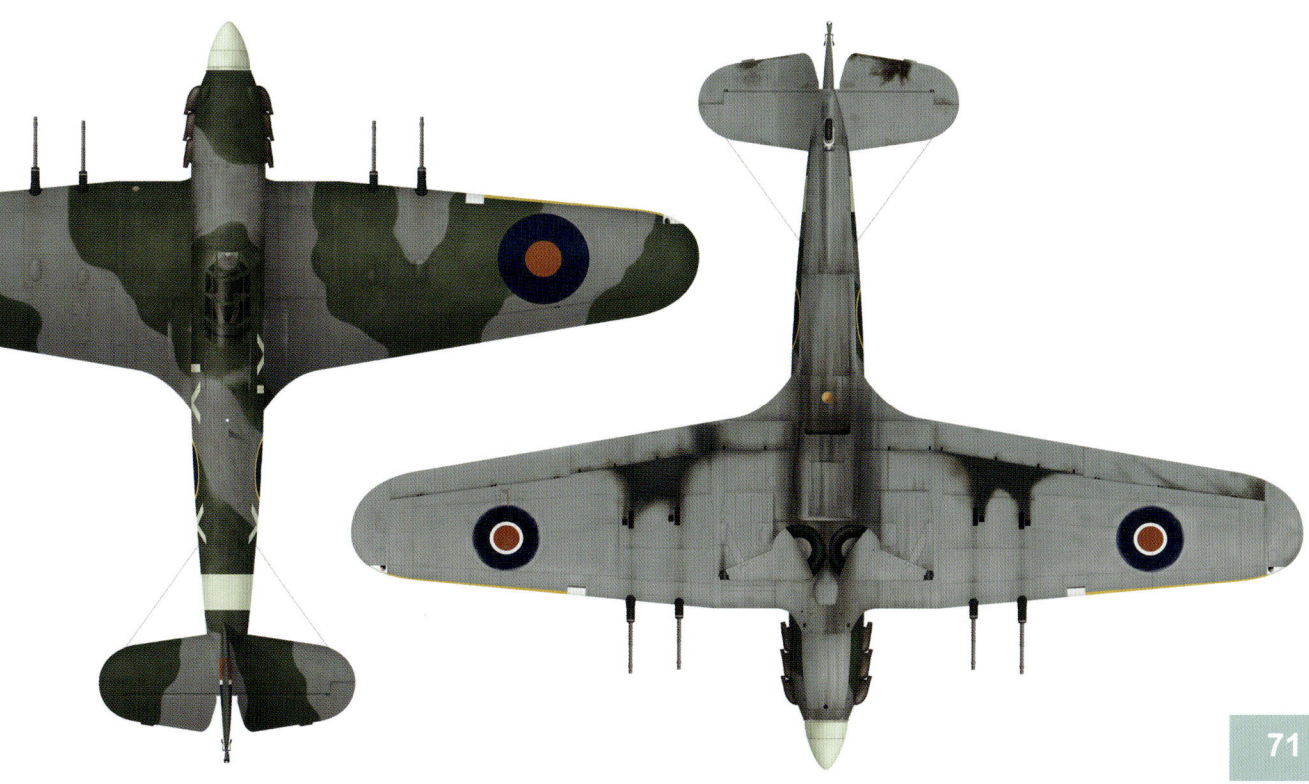

Discussion points

• Fitted with a 'pointed' Rotol CM/1 propeller spinner and 'Jablo' propeller blades.
• Armed with four Mk 1 Hispano 20mm cannon with 'flat' recoil springs.
• The four wing leading edge cannon fairings are still in Special Night.
• Early style exhaust manifolds.
• Dowty oil-spring oleo 'straight' leg tailwheel.
• Sky rear fuselage band truncated along the upper/under surface demarcation line.
• Crudely applied upper and under surface colours wearing off to the rear of the cartridge case ejection chutes and around the radiator.

A trio of 1 Squadron Hurricane Mk IIcs, (presumably photographed over Northumberland during the same photo shoot as the previous pages). JX•I HL603 is in the factory applied scheme and JX•J and JX•H BD946 have the squadron applied camouflage.